# A-LEVEL C

# FLASH NOTES

# OCR A Year 1 and AS

## New Syllabus 2015

Dr C. Boes

Condensed Revision Notes (Flashcards) for a
Successful Exam Preparation

Designed to Facilitate Memorization

For revision tips and special offers go to:

www.alevelchemistryrevision.co.uk

Self-published 2016

ISBN-13: 978-0-9957060-0-2

# Contents

# How to use these notes

These revision notes are organized in chapters according to the current OCR A Year 1 & AS syllabus (from Sept 2015). Each chapter contains individual revision cards covering all the necessary topics. Everything in *italic* is optional knowledge, aimed at students who want to excel or want to continue to year 2. **Bold** represents important keywords or key definitions. 'Data sheet' indicates information which will be provided on the data sheet or in the question during the exam and does not need to be memorized. Important information and exam-specific tips are highlighted in yellow.

**How to memorize:** The revision cards are introduced by their titles and keywords on a separate page. After reading the title you should try to write down the content of the card without looking at the next page. The keywords give you hints about the content. Write down everything you remember, even if you are not sure. Then check if your answers are correct; if not, rewrite the incorrect ones.

At the beginning, when you are still unfamiliar with the cards, it might help to read them a few times first. If they contain a lot of content, you can cover the revision card with a piece of paper and slowly reveal the header and sub content. While you uncover it try to remember what is written in the covered part, e.g. the definition for a term you just uncovered. This uncovering technique is for the early stages, later you should be able to write down the whole content after just reading the header. If this is the case, move to the next card. If not, bookmark the card and memorize it repeatedly. Do at least four to five sessions per week until you know all the cards of one chapter word-perfectly. When you have memorized a revision card apply your new knowledge by answering topic questions. Then move on to the next section. Generally it is better to do shorter sessions more often than longer sessions less frequently. An even better option is to ask somebody to check your knowledge by reading the header aloud and comparing your answer to the content.

## Exam techniques

Begin with a quick look through the exam. How is it structured; what topics are coming up and how many questions are there? Then work systematically through it from the beginning, but keep an eye on the time. When you fall behind shorten your answers and leave difficult topics for the end.

Underline or highlight the important information/data in the question. If just names for compounds are given, write the chemical formula above it (e.g. sulfuric acid -> $H_2SO_4$).

Circle the functional groups in an organic formula and name them. Draw the carbons and hydrogens in skeletal formulae or displayed formulae if the structural formulae are given.

Make sure you read the question thoroughly and be aware what actions are expected from you from the command words used.

Identify the topic of the question and mentally bring up the flashcards associated to the topic. They will help you with the answer. If you have problems understanding the question, read it again slowly and also read through the follow up sub-questions (a, b, c etc.) sometimes the topic and the initial question becomes clearer. If you still do not understand the question or cannot come up with all the answers, do not spend any more time on it. Write down your best answers or just standard keywords/phrases from the flashcard. Writing something is better than writing nothing. You might still get some marks for it. Circle the question and come back to it at the end of the exam.

If you do calculations, write down a list of the data given (time permitting – otherwise just underline) and the formulae/equations which you are using (even if your calculation is wrong, you might get a mark for the correct formula).

Always show your workings and do the unit calculations. This means writing the units next to the numbers and cancelling or multiplying them accordingly. You should get the correct unit for your final answer. If not, you might not have converted them correctly (e.g. $cm^3$ into $dm^3$) or have used the wrong equation.

After writing down the final answer check if it makes sense (is the number in the expected range; does it have the correct sign in front, e. g. – for an exothermic reaction etc.).

Calculation answers should always be given in decimals, never fractions. Furthermore make sure you have answered all the questions and everything asked for (e.g. state symbols, significant figures etc.)

For multiple choice questions: read all answers and strike through the ones which are definitely wrong. Choose the correct or most likely of the remaining ones. If you have no clue take the longest answer. Always choose an answer -> you have at least a 25 % chance to get it right :-).

Do not spend too much time on a question. Rule of thumb is 1 min per mark. If you are unsure, circle the question and come back to it at the end of the exam.

More tips about how to plan your revision and how to prepare for exams can be found on my website: https://www.alevelchemistryrevision.co.uk

**Disclaimer:** Due to the changing nature of mark schemes it cannot be guaranteed that answering according to these notes will give you full marks. These notes constitute only one part of a full revision program and work alongside other methods, like practising past papers. They have been created with great care; however, errors or omissions cannot be excluded. They are designed for the final stage of revision and require a thorough understanding of the topics.

# Module 1 – Development of Practical Skills (Paper 1 & 2) H032

## 1.1 Practical Skills Assessed in a Written Examination

# Accuracy and Reliability
# &
# Uncertainty
# &
# Independent and Dependent Variables

Definition of accuracy

Definition of reliability and three points

Definition of uncertainty

Two points about uncertainty

Equation of percentage error

Tip to decrease percentage error

Definitions of independent and dependent variables

Example

## Accuracy and Reliability (Practical)

**Accuracy:** how close the result is to the true value

**Reliability:** How reproducible the result is
- The more times an experiment is repeated the more reliable the result
- This reduces effect of **random errors** (e.g. limitation of accuracy of pipette: getting 49.9 ml or 50.1 ml when measuring 50 ml)
- But the result can still be wrong due to a **systematic error** (e.g. wrong calibration of a balance -> always 0.5 g to heavy)

## Uncertainty (Practical)

**Definition:** The uncertainty in a single measurement from a single instrument is **half the least count (unit) of the instrument**

-> add uncertainties of each reading *(and instrument)* together
-> uncertainties are due to the limits of **sensitivity** of the instrument

$$\text{Percentage error} = \frac{\text{Uncertainty}}{\text{Reading}} \times 100$$

To decrease percentage error, increase value of reading, e.g. use larger volume or mass (or decrease uncertainty by using more sensitive equipment)

**Example:**
- burette with 0.1 ml graduation => +/- 0.05 ml (maximum error)
  -> 0.05 ml uncertainty
- two readings (before and after titration) two times uncertainty
  2 x 0.05 ml = 0.1 ml total uncertainty for the titration
- if 10 ml of standard solution was used for the titration then uncertainty:
  0.1 ml/10 ml = 1.0 % of this volume reading

## Independent and Dependent Variables (Practical)

**Independent variable:** the variable (value) the scientist changes to see what effect it has -> cause (x-axis)

**Dependent variable:** the variable (value) the scientist measures to see what the result of changing the independent variable is -> effect (y-axis)
*This value depends on the independent variable, therefore called 'dependent'*

**Example:** The scientist wants to know if the volume of hydrogen gas produced depends on the mass of metal used for the following reaction:

$$Mg + H_2SO_4 \rightarrow MgSO_4 + H_2$$

He weights different masses of Mg (2 g, 4 g, 6 g, 8 g => independent variable) and measures the volume of the gas produced (5, 10, 15, 20 $cm^3$ => dependent variable). He makes a table of his results and plots a graph, which shows an ascending line. He concludes the volume depends on the mass.

# Module 2 – Foundations in Chemistry (Paper 1 & 2)

## 2.1 Atoms and Reactions

## 2.1.1 Atomic Structures and Isotopes

# Basic Definitions

Atom

Table of subatomic particles

Element

Isotopes

Atomic number

Mass number

Ion

Relative atomic mass with equation

Relative isotopic mass

Molar mass

Relative molecular mass

## Basic Definitions

**Atom:** smallest unit of an element
-> consist of electrons organized in orbitals/shells and a nucleus made from protons and neutrons

| Subatomic Particle | Relative mass | Charge |
|---|---|---|
| Proton | 1 | +1 |
| Neutron | 1 | 0 |
| Electron | 1/2000 | -1 |

**Element:** same kind of atoms (same atomic number)

**Isotopes:** atoms with same number of protons but different number of neutrons
*(same element: same atomic number but different mass number)*

**Atomic number:** number of protons (equals number of electrons)

**Mass number:** protons + neutrons

**Ion: charged particle** (different numbers of protons and electrons)
positive -> **cation** (more protons than electrons)
negative -> **anion** (more electrons than protons)
=> *formed when an atom gains or loses electrons to get a full outer shell*

**Relative Atomic mass $A_r$**
Is the average (weighted) mass of an element's isotopes (atoms) relative to 1/12 the mass of a $^{12}C$ atom [no unit]

$$A_r = \frac{(a\% \times A_1) + (b\% \times A_2)}{100}$$

a%: percentage of Isotope 1
b%: percentage of Isotope 2
$A_1$: Relative Isotopic mass of Isotope 1
$A_2$: Relative Isotopic mass of Isotope 2

=> $A_r$ and **Relative Isotopic Abundance** can be worked out from a Mass Spectrum ($A_1, A_2$ from x-axis and a%, b% from y-axis of each peak)
-> see revision card 'Mass Spectrometry'

**Relative isotopic mass**
Is the mass of an atom of an isotope relative to 1/12 the mass of a $^{12}C$ atom [no unit]

**Molar mass M**
Mass of one mole of a substance [g $mol^{-1}$]

**Relative molecular Mass $M_r$ (relative formula mass)**
of a compound is the sum of the relative atomic masses of all its atoms [no unit]

# 2.1.2 Compounds, Formulae and Equations

# List of Anions
# &
# Naming Salts

Ten anions

Rule for writing chemical formulae of salts

Rule for naming cations

Four rules for naming anions

## List of Anions

| | |
|---|---|
| chloride | $Cl^-$ |
| carbonate | $CO_3^{2-}$ |
| hydroxide | $OH^-$ |
| sulphate | $SO_4^{2-}$ |
| sulphate(IV)/*sulphite* | $SO_3^{2-}$ |
| sulphide | $S^{2-}$ |
| nitrate | $NO_3^-$ |
| phosphate | $PO_4^{3-}$ |
| ethanoate/*acetate* | $CH_3COO^-$ |
| cyanide | $CN^-$ |


## Naming Salts (Systematic Name)

First cation (metal, +) then anion (non-metal, -): e.g. NaCl -> sodium chloride

**Cation (positive ion)**
Oxidation number of the cation is written in roman numerals in brackets in the salt name to distinguish different salts,
e.g. Iron(II) sulphate: $FeSO_4$; Iron(III) sulphate: $Fe_2(SO_4)_3$

**Anion (negative ion)**
Name of anion finishes with:

- ide      anion consists of just one element like $S^{2-}$,
            e.g. CaS – calcium sulph**ide** or NaCl – sodium chlor**ide**

- ate      anion consists of more than one elements like $SO_4^{2-}$ (sulphur & oxygen) and sulphur is in its highest oxidation state (+6),
            e.g. $Na_2SO_4$ – Sodium sulph**ate** -> or **sulphate(VI)**

- ate(IV)  anion with more than one element (sulphur & oxygen) and sulphur is in a lower oxidation state (+4):
            **write oxidation state as roman numeral in brackets**
            for example $Na_2SO_3$ – Sodium **sulphate(IV)**
            **=> use this as general method for naming anions with more than one element**

- *ite*      *anion with more than one element (sulphur & oxygen) and sulphur is in its second highest oxidation state (+4) -> old way of naming; for example $Na_2SO_3$ – Sodium sulf**ite** -> or **sulphate(IV)***

# Mole
# &
# Molar Gas Volume

Mole: Definition and equation

Equation for calculating number of particles

Molar gas volume at standard conditions

Equation for calculating volume of gas from moles

Converting $cm^3$ into $dm^3$

Ideal gas equation with SI units

Two Tips

# Mole

**Def.: 1 mole** = $6.02 \times 10^{23}$ **particles** (atoms, molecules, ions, electrons etc.)
-> Avogadro's number $N_A$, *see data sheet*

$$n = \frac{m}{M_r}$$

n:   number of moles [moles]
m:   mass [g]
$M_r$: molar mass [g/mol]
[ ]:   units

## Number of particles

$$N = n \times N_A$$

N:   number of particles [no unit]
$N_A$: Avogadro's number $6.02 \times 10^{23}$ [$mol^{-1}$]


## Molar Gas Volume

Volume of **1 mole** of any **gas** = *24 dm³ (data sheet)*
-> at **standard conditions (298 K/25 °C, 100 kPa)**

$$V_x = n \times 24 \text{ dm}^3 \text{ mol}^{-1}$$

$V_x$: unknown volume [$dm^3$]
n:   number of moles [moles]

**Converting $cm^3$ into $dm^3$:**

$$x \text{ cm}^3 = \frac{x}{1000} \text{ dm}^3$$

**Ideal gas equation:**

$$pV = nRT$$

p:   pressure **[Pa]**
V:   volume **[m³]**                    $1 \text{ m}^3 = 1000 \text{ dm}^3$
R:   *8.31* J $K^{-1}$ $mol^{-1}$ (gas constant) -> *data sheet*
T:   temperature **[K]**                   (K = 273 + °C)

-> **make sure you are using correct SI units - see [ ]**

-> the ratios of the volumes of reactants and products can be used to work out the mole equation (reaction equation):
**Volumes are proportional to moles**

# Empirical and Molecular Formulae

Definitions of molecular and empirical formulae

Relationships between these formulae for salts and molecules

Work out empirical formulae from masses (three points)

Empirical Formulae from percentages (one point)

Molecular formulae from empirical formulae and molecular mass

Example Calculation

## Empirical and Molecular Formulae

**Molecular formula: Actual number of atoms** (of each type of element) in a molecule, e.g. Ethene $C_2H_4$ => closer to reality; generally used in equations.

**Empirical formula: Smallest whole number ratio** of atoms (of each element) in a compound; $CH_2$ => Empirical formula is used when trying to find out the molecular formula of an unknown organic compound by burning it.

- For Salts: chemical formula is identical with empirical formula
- For Molecules: molecular formula is a multiple of empirical formula

**Work out empirical formulae from masses (burning hydrocarbon):**
- Use n=m/M to calculate moles of each element; take mole ratios into account, e.g. H in $H_2O$ 2 : 1
- If organic compound contains O, subtract masses of C and H from total mass to get mass of O.
- Divide by smallest mole number to get ratio (empirical formula)

**How to work out empirical formulae from percentages:**
- Change percentages into grams, then same as above.

**Work out molecular formulae from empirical formulae and molecular mass**
- Divide molecular $M_r$ by empirical $M_r$ to get factor
- Multiply empirical formula with factor to get molecular formula

## Example calculation

When an unknown hydrocarbon with $M_r = 70$ g/mol is burnt in excess oxygen, we get **6.6 g** of $CO_2$ and **2.7 g** of $H_2O$ (elemental analysis).
What is the empirical and molecular formula of this compound?

**Calculate empirical formula first**
**Moles $CO_2$:**
n = **6.6 g**/44 g/mol = 0.15 mol (1 mole C in 1 mole $CO_2$ -> factor 1)
=> **Moles C:** n = **0.15 mol**

**Moles $H_2O$:**
n = 2.7 g/18 g mol$^{-1}$ = 0.15 mol (2 mole H in 1 mole $H_2O$ -> factor 2)
=> **Moles H:** n = 2 x 0.15 mol = **0.3 mol**

Divide by smallest mole number:
**C** 0.15/0.15 = 1, **H** 0.3/0.15 = 2
Ratio     **C : H**     1 : 2
**Empirical formula: $C_1H_2$ => $CH_2$**

**Calculate Molecular formula from Mr and empirical formula**
Unknown hydrocarbon          $M_r = 70$ g mol$^{-1}$
Empirical molar mass $CH_2$          $M_r = 14$ g mol$^{-1}$
Factor:          70 g mol$^{-1}$/ 14 g mol$^{-1}$= 5
**Molecular formula:**          5 x $CH_2$ => $C_5H_{10}$ => Pentene

# Water of Crystallisation

Explanation of two terms

Three characteristics of water of crystallisation

Experiment to determine water of crystallisation (two points)

Example Calculation

# Water of crystallisation

## Terms

**Anhydrous salt** -> no water

**Hydrated salt** -> water incorporated in lattice

- Water of crystallisation is expressed with dot and mole number in chemical formula
  -> **water is included in molar mass $M_r$** and belongs to the compound.
  => the number of moles $H_2O$ per mole salt is written in the formula:
  $Na_2CO_3 \cdot 10H_2O$   $M_r = 286$ g/mol $(2\times23 + 12 + 3\times16 + \mathbf{10\times18})$

## Experiment to determine water of crystallisation

- when heated hydrated salts lose water of crystallisation and become lighter (anhydrous) -> heat to constant mass
- difference in mass is due to the water lost and can be used to calculate the number of moles of water of crystallisation in the chemical formula (**X**):
  -> Calculate moles $H_2O$ and moles anhydrous salt by using $n = m/M$
  -> Divide moles of $H_2O$ by moles of anhydrous salt to get **X**
  -> Similar to calculating empirical formulas

## Example Calculation

When **6.42 g** of **hydrated magnesium sulphate, $MgSO_4 \cdot XH_2O$** is heated **3.14 g** of **anhydrous magnesium sulphate** is left. What is the formula of the hydrated salt, e.g. **X**?

**Water lost:** 6.42 g – 3.14 g = 3.28 g

**Moles $H_2O$:**  n = 3.28 g/18 g mol$^{-1}$ = **0.182 moles**

**Moles $MgSO_4$:** n = 3.14 g/120.4 g mol$^{-1}$ 1 = **0.0261 moles**

$X = 0.182$ mole / $0.0261$ mole $= 6.95 = 7$

=> $MgSO_4 \cdot 7H_2O$

# Mole Equations – Calculate Masses
# &
# Percentage Yield

Calculation Steps

Rule for rounding

Rules for significant figures

Example

Equation for percentage yield

Units

Tip

Four reasons for loss

## Mole Equations – Calculate Masses

1) Underline or highlight all data given in the exam question.
2) Calculate moles for the given compound by using $n = m/M$.
3) Circle or highlight mole numbers in front of related compounds (given and unknown).
4) Determine mole ratio for unknown compound.
5) Get mole factor by dividing both mole numbers by the same number (here: 4) so that the given compound becomes 1.
6) Multiply moles of given compound with factor to get moles of unknown compound.
7) Calculate mass of unknown compound by using $m = n \times M$.
8) Do not round whilst still calculating. Carry as many digits through the calculation as possible (at least 3) until you reach the final answer.
9) Write the answer with the appropriate number of significant figures: if the data are given in 3 significant figures then the answer should also be given in 3 significant figures (see below).
10) If the data are given in 2 and 3 significant figures then the answer should be given in 2 significant figures (always the lowest one).
11) The first significant figure is the first digit which is not zero: 0.0109.
12) If the last non-significant figure is 1 - 4 round down, if 5 – 9 round up.
13) $0.001 = 1 \times 10^{-3}$ -> use standard form for scientific calculations.

### Example

1) Calculate amount of $O_2$ (in grams) produced if 3.24 g of iron(III) nitrate is heated

$$4Fe(NO_3)_3 -> 2Fe_2O_3 + 12NO_2 + 3O_2$$

2) Moles $Fe(NO_3)_3$ : $n = 3.24$ g$/ 241.8$ g/mol $= 0.0134$ moles
3) See mole equation above
4) Ratio: 3 : 4
5) Factor for $O_2$: ¾ = 0.75 ($Fe(NO_3)_3$ : $4/4 = 1$)
6) Moles $O_2$ : $0.75 \times 0.0134$ moles $= 0.01005$ moles
7) Mass $O_2$: $m = n \times M = 0.01005$ mol $\times 32$ g/mol $= 0.322$ g

## Percentage Yield

percentage yield = $\dfrac{\text{actual yield}}{\text{theoretical yield}}$ x 100

units of actual/theoretical yield of desired **products**: [grams] or [moles]

-> **make sure actual and theoretical yield of products are in the same unit**

### Reasons for loss

- Reaction not complete (clumps instead of powder)
- Loss of product (sticking to vessel, evaporation of liquids)
- By-products
- Impurities of reactants

# Atom Economy
# &
# Concentrations

Equation for atom economy and four points

Benefits of high atom economy (four points)

Example calculation

Equation for mole concentration

Converting $dm^3$ in $cm^3$

Equation for mass concentration

Converting mole concentration into mass concentration

## Atom Economy

$$\% \text{ atom economy } = \frac{M_r \text{ desired product}}{\Sigma M_r \text{ all products}} \times 100$$

$\Sigma$: sum

- **100 % for addition reactions (no waste products)**
- **multiply $M_r$ with mole numbers from chemical equation**
- high atom economy indicates high efficiency
- unwanted by-products lower atom economy

**Environmental and economic benefits of high atom economy**
- Avoiding waste
- High sustainability (less raw material)
- More profitable (raw material and removal of waste products expensive)
- High efficiency

**Example calculation**

$$(NH_4)_2SO_{4(s)} + 2NaOH_{(aq)} \rightarrow 2NH_{3(g)} + Na_2SO_{4(aq)} + 2H_2O_{(l)}$$

**Calculate the percentage atom economy for the production of ammonia**

$$\% \text{ atom economy } = \frac{2 \times 17}{2 \times 17 + 142 + 2 \times 18} \times 100$$

$$= 16.0 \%$$

## Concentration

**Mole concentration:**

$$c = \frac{n}{V}$$

n:  moles [mol]
V:  volume [$dm^3$]
c:  concentration [mol $dm^{-3}$]

**1 $dm^3$ = 1000 $cm^3$**

**Mass concentration:**

$$c_m = \frac{m}{V}$$

m:  mass [g]
c:  mass concentration [g $dm^{-3}$]

**Convert mole concentration into mass concentration:**

$$c_m = M_r \times c$$

# 2.1.4 Acids

# Acids
# &
# Bases

Definition of acid

Five important acids

Reaction with metals

Reaction with alkali

Difference between strong and weak acids

Definition of base

Four types of bases

Acid test

(Limewater test)

Definition of alkali

Two tests for acids & bases

(Two rules for anions)

## Acids

**Definition (Bronsted-Lowry): proton ($H^+$) donor**
*Arrhenius: releases $H^+$ (base: $OH^-$); Lavoisier: contains oxygen -> Year 2*

**Important acids:**

| | |
|---|---|
| HCl | hydrochloric acid (hydrogen chloride) - s |
| $H_2SO_4$ | sulphuric acid - s |
| $HNO_3$ | nitric acid - s |
| $H_2CO_3$ | carbonic acid - w |
| $CH_3COOH$ | ethanoic acid, *acetic acid* - w |

**Acids reacting with metals forming hydrogen and a salt (Redox)**
$$Mg + H_2SO_4 \rightarrow MgSO_4 + H_2 \qquad \text{Fizzing, } \textbf{Mg disappears}$$

**Acids reacting with alkali forming water and a salt -> see Hydroxides below**

**Strong acids (s):** Completely dissociated:
$$HCl \ \rightarrow \ H^+ + Cl^-$$

**Weak acids (w):** Partially dissociated:
$$CH_3COOH \ \rightleftharpoons \ CH_3COO^- + H^+$$
=> equilibrium (less $H^+$ ions)

## Bases (Practical)

**-> Proton ($H^+$) acceptor**

**Metal oxides (s) (Acid-Base Reaction)**
$$\textbf{MgO} + 2HCl \rightarrow MgCl_2 + H_2O \qquad \textbf{Indigestion tablets}$$

**Hydroxides (s)**
$$\textbf{Ca(OH)}_2 + 2HCl \rightarrow CaCl_2 + 2H_2O \qquad \textbf{Neutralises acid soils; Removes HCl-fumes}$$

**Ammonia (w)**
$$\textbf{NH}_3 + HCl \rightarrow NH_4Cl \qquad \text{Fertilizer}$$

**Carbonates (w)**
$$\textbf{CaCO}_{3(s)} + 2HCl \rightarrow CaCl_2 + H_2O + CO_2 \qquad \text{Fizzing, } \textbf{CaCO}_3 \textbf{ disappears}$$
=> **acid test**

Test for $CO_2$ **(limewater test):** see revision card 'Test for Ions'.

**Alkali:** A soluble base: base that dissolves in water and **releases $OH^-$**.

**Tests for acids and bases:**
- pH indicator changes colour (litmus red -> blue base; blue -> red acid).
- pH meter shows value lower (acid) or greater (base) than **7**.

*-> Anion of weak acid is a base (-> conjugated base).*
*-> Anion of strong acid is **not** a base.*

---

# Acids and Bases Preparation
# &
# Preparing a Standard Solution

Preparing acids with word and symbol equations (three points)

Preparing bases with word and symbol equations (one point)

Steps for preparing a standard solution

## Acids and Bases Preparation

**Acids:**

| Non-metal-oxide | + water -> | Acid |
|---|---|---|
| $CO_2$ | $+ H_2O$ -> | $H_2CO_3$ |

-> Non-metal-oxides are hidden acids
-> **$CO_2$ from the air can make solutions acidic**
-> **$SO_2$ causes acid rain** (removed by CaO in scrubbers: $CaO + SO_2 -> CaSO_3$)

**Bases:**

| Metaloxide | + water -> | Metalhydroxide |
|---|---|---|
| CaO | $+ H_2O$ -> | $Ca(OH)_2$ |

-> Metal oxides are hidden hydroxides/bases

## Preparing a Standard Solution (Practical)

- calculate moles of compound from volume and concentration using $n = c\ V$
- calculate mass of compound by using $m = n\ M$
- place a plastic weighing boat (dish) or weighing paper on a digital **balance** and zero the balance (tare)
- weigh the compound to an appropriate number of decimal places (e.g. 0.01)
- *if the solid compound has been stored in the fridge allow it to reach room temperature before opening the bottle*
- transfer the compound into a beaker which already contains some solvent (distilled $H_2O$) -> around 80 % of the final volume (e.g. 80 ml of 100 ml final volume)
- the solvent should be at room temperature
- rinse the weighing boat with distilled water to transfer the remaining compound, sticking to the boat, into the beaker
- completely dissolve by stirring the mixture, of compound and solvent, in the beaker
- if it's necessary to heat or cool to aid dissolving, ensure the solution has reached room temperature before the next step
- transfer the solution to a **volumetric flask** using a funnel
- rinse the beaker and stirrer and add the washing water into the flask
- slowly add distilled water up to the calibration mark of the flask (bottom of the meniscus)
- insert stopper and shake thoroughly to ensure complete mixing
- label the flask

# Titrations

Purpose

Function of Indicator (two points)

Two indicators with their colour changes

Endpoint

Choices of indicators for three different titrations

Titration steps

Accuracy of volume measurement

## Titrations (Practical)

-> method to determine a concentration

### Acid-Base Titration (Neutralisation)

**Indicator** *(weak organic acid)*
- indicates pH jump by colour change at endpoint
- pH range over which indicator changes colour is approximately two pH units *(pK$_a$ +/- 1)* -> *changes from protonated to deprotonated form (Y2)*

| | | |
|---|---|---|
| **phenolphthalein:** | colourless (a) | -> pink (b) |
| **methyl orange:** | red (a) | -> yellow (b) |
| not universal indicator | -> too gradual colour change | |

**Endpoint, equivalence point** (same number of moles of H$^+$ & OH$^-$)
-> pH of indicator colour change *(pka)* must match equivalence point:
- Weak base with strong acid -> methyl orange *(pka = 3.5)*
- Weak acid with strong base -> phenolphthalein *(pka = 9.3)*
- Strong acid with strong base -> any indicator

### Titration Steps

- Flush burette with distilled H$_2$O and standard solution (water dilutes standard)
- fill burette with standard solution above 0 and drain to 0 mark (removes air bubbles in tap)
- fill exact volume of unknown solution, with volumetric pipette, in conical flask
- add few drops of indicator (too much indicator would change pH)
- use white tile as background (to better see the colour change).
- do rough titration to get an idea for the endpoint: add solution & swirl until colour change
- do accurate titration and repeat at least three times (reliability)
- record volumes of standard solution used (eyes level, bottom of meniscus, to the nearest 0.05 cm$^3$)
- calculate the average volume (ignore values which do not match: > 0.1 cm$^3$)
- calculate moles of standard solution from this volume using n = c V
- take mole ratios from reaction equation into account: if a **polyprotic** acid has been titrated with a **monoprotic** standard solution, divide moles of standard solution by proton number (e.g. diprotic H$_2$SO$_4$, divide by 2)
- calculate concentration of unknown solution by using c = n/V

### Accuracy of volume measurement

volumetric pipette > graduated pipette > burette > measuring cylinder

## 2.1.5 Redox

# Redox Reactions – Oxidation States
# &
# Disproportionation

Definitions of Oxidation and Reduction

Purpose of oxidation states

Six rules for oxidation states including list of most common states

Oxidising/Reducing agent

Tip

Definition of disproportionation with example

## Redox Reactions – Oxidation States

Oxidation Is Loss of electrons
-> oxidation state becomes more positive

Reduction Is Gain of electrons
-> oxidation state becomes more negative

=> OILRIG

### Oxidation states/numbers
-> help to determine chemical formula of compound

*Def:* *identical to the charges of ions in a salt;*
*the charge an element would have, in a molecule, if it were a salt.*

**Rules:**
- always zero for pure element in its basic state (uncombined element)
- group number indicates **maximum** oxidation state
- the more electronegative element gets a negative -, the less electronegative element a positive oxidation number
- the sum of all oxidation states for neutral compounds is zero
  $Al_2O_3$        $(2x+3) + (3x-2) = 0$
  $\phantom{Al_2}{}_{+3}\phantom{O}{}_{-2}$
- the sum of all oxidation states for ions equals their charge
  $SO_4^{2-}$        $(+6) + (4x-2) = -2$
  $\phantom{S}{}_{+6}\phantom{O_4}{}_{-2}$
- most common oxidation states in compounds:
  Halogens   -1
  Oxygen     -2 (-1 peroxides)
  Hydrogen   +1 (-1)
  Metals positive (alkali metals +1, alkaline earth metals +2)

**Oxidising agent**: gets reduced (helps other element to get oxidised)
-> **electron acceptors**

**Reducing agent**: gets oxidised (helps other element to get reduced)
-> **electron donors**

Oxidising/Reducing agent is the whole compound not just the element which changes oxidation state

### Disproportionation

**Definition: same element gets reduced and oxidized**

-> Special kind of Redox reaction

$Cu_2O + 2H^+ \rightarrow Cu^{2+} + Cu + H_2O$
$\phantom{Cu_2}{}_{+1} \phantom{+ 2H^+ \rightarrow} {}_{+2} \phantom{Cu^{2+} + Cu} {}_{0}$

-> see also revision card 'Water Treatment'

# Balancing Redox Equations

Balancing a simple redox reaction (two points)

Balancing a complicated redox reaction (two points)

Two important rules for balancing redox reactions

(Half equations)

## Balancing Redox Equations

### How to balance a simple redox equation

- First write the chemical formula of the product to the right side of the arrow. Balance this formula with subscript numbers according to oxidation states (group number) by using lowest common multiple.
- Then balance equation by putting numbers in front of partners (never change subscript numbers, as this would create a different substance)

$$4Al + 3O_2 \rightarrow 2Al_2O_3$$
$$\phantom{4Al}_{0} \phantom{+ 3O}_{0} \phantom{\rightarrow 2Al_2}_{+3 \ -2} \quad \text{(lowest common multiple: 6)}$$

### If not just elements reacting (ions/molecules):

- First balance electrons, starting with the biggest difference in oxidation states (between left and right side of equation)
- then balance all the other reactants and products *(single elements like sulphur first; oxygen before hydrogen)*

$$8I^- + 8H^+ + H_2SO_4 \rightarrow 4I_2 + H_2S + 4H_2O$$
$$\phantom{8I}_{-1} \phantom{+ 8H^+ + H_2S}_{+6} \phantom{\rightarrow 4I_2}_{0} \phantom{+H_2}_{-2}$$

Biggest difference: S: $+6 \rightarrow -2$     => gains $8e^-$
I: $-1 \rightarrow 0$ => loses $1e^-$ => $8I^-$ needed ($\rightarrow 4I_2$)

- number of electrons **lost and gained must be the same!**
- charges have to be balanced as well ($8I^- = 8H^+$)


## *Half-Equations (Year 2)*

- *half equations split up redox reaction in two separate oxidation and reduction reactions*
- *use oxidation states to determine number of transferred electrons*
- *number of electrons transferred must be the same in overall equation -> multiply to get lowest common multiple (here: 6)*

$$3Zn + 2Fe^{3+} \rightarrow 2Fe + 3Zn^{2+}$$
$$\phantom{3Zn}_{0} \phantom{+ 2Fe}_{+3} \phantom{\rightarrow 2Fe}_{0} \phantom{+ 3Zn}_{+2}$$

*half equations:*
$$Fe^{3+} + 3e^- \rightarrow Fe \qquad\qquad | \ x\ 2$$
$$Zn \rightarrow Zn^{2+} + 2e^- \qquad\quad | \ x\ 3$$

- *Sometimes $H^+$ or $H_2O$ have to be added to half-equation to balance them*
- *see also Year 2 revision card 'Redox Equations'*

# Two Main Types of Inorganic Reactions
# &
# Ionic Equations

Two main types

Tip

Two minor types

Four state symbols

Tip

Definition of spectator ion

## Two Main Types of Inorganic Reactions

### 1) Redox (Reduction/Oxidation)

-> transfer of electrons (Oxidation states change)

$$4Al + 3O_2 -> 2Al_2O_3$$
$$\phantom{4Al}_{0} \phantom{+ 3}_{0} \phantom{-> 2Al_2O}_{+3} \phantom{}_{-2}$$

-> **Displacement** & **Disproportionation** are special cases of Redox reactions

**You can quickly spot a redox reaction if an element becomes an ion or part of a compound and visa versa in a reaction equation (see above)**

### 2) Acid-Base (Neutralisation)

-> transfer of protons $H^+$ (Oxidation states do not change)

$$HCl + NaOH -> NaCl + H_2O$$
$$\phantom{H}_{+1} \phantom{}_{-1} \phantom{+ N}_{+1} \phantom{aO}_{-2} \phantom{H}_{+1} \phantom{-> N}_{+1} \phantom{a}_{-1} \phantom{Cl + H}_{+1} \phantom{}_{-2}$$

### Minor reaction types

- Thermal decomposition
  $$CaCO_{3(s)} -> CaO_{(s)} + CO_{2(g)}$$

- Precipitation
  $$Ag^+_{(aq)} + Cl^-_{(aq)} -> AgCl_{(s)}$$

-> No change of oxidation states

### State Symbols

$s$ = solid, $l$ = liquid, $g$ = gas, $aq$ = aqueous (solution in water)

**If the melting or boiling point is below room temperature (25 °C, 298 K) then the substance is a liquid or a gas respectively.**

### Ionic Equations

-> only show the reacting particles

**Spectator Ions:** Ions which do not take part in the reaction
They can be removed from the full equation to give an ionic equation

Full equation:
$$Cl_2 + 2NaBr -> Br_2 + 2NaCl$$
$$\phantom{Cl}_{0} \phantom{+ 2Na}_{+1} \phantom{B}_{-1} \phantom{-> B}_{0} \phantom{r_2 + 2Na}_{+1} \phantom{C}_{-1}$$

$Na^+$ does not change oxidation states -> spectator ion, removed from equation:

**Ionic equation:**
$$Cl_2 + 2Br^- -> Br_2 + 2Cl^-$$
$$\phantom{Cl}_{0} \phantom{+ 2B}_{-1} \phantom{-> B}_{0} \phantom{r_2 + 2C}_{-1}$$

# 2.2 Electrons, Bonding and Structure

## 2.2.1 Electron Structure

# Electron Configuration

Function of Electron Configuration

Definition of orbital

Four rules

Meaning of the numbers & letters

Electron configuration and box diagram for Nitrogen

Shapes of s- and p-orbitals

Table of subshells (s, p, d, f)

Equation for number of electrons per shell

## Electron Configuration

-> **Distribution of electrons across the shells and subshells of an atom**

**Orbitals**

**Definition: Region of space in which electrons are most likely to be found; one orbital can hold up to two electrons, which must have opposite spins.**
- Electrons fill up the lowest energy shells/subshells first
- Orbitals of the same subshell are filled individually first (electrons repel)
- 4s get emptied and filled before 3d (see revision card 'Transition Metals')
- For cations take off electrons, for anions add electrons according to charge
- Number of electrons per shell: $2n^2$      n: shell number

N: $1s^2 2s^2 2p^3$          [He] $2s^2 2p^3$

    **2: shell (principal quantum number)**
    **p: subshell**
    **3: number of electrons (in subshell)**

**Box diagram:**

Electronic configuration of N

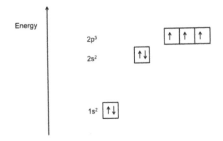

**Shapes of orbitals:**

    s-orbital:                      p-orbital:

    Sphere                      Dumbbell

| Subshells | Orbitals | Electrons |
|---|---|---|
| s | 1 | 2 |
| p | 3 | 6 |
| d | 5 | 10 |
| f | 7 | 14 |

## 2.2.2 Bonding and Structure


# Ionic and Covalent Compounds and Bonds


Definition of compound

Names and Characteristics of ionic compounds (four points)

Three physical properties

Two examples

Definition of ionic bond

Draw lattice


Names and Characteristics of covalent compounds (four points)

Three physical properties

Two examples

Definition of covalent bond

Definition & symbol of dative covalent bond

## Ionic and Covalent Compounds and Bonds

**Compound:** Atoms of different elements bonded together

**Ionic compounds - Salts: Metal/Non-metal**
- Consist of ions
- 'Dot-and Cross' diagram: square bracket with charge around ion
- Form lattice with alternating charges (see diagram below)
- Chemical formula gives ratio (ion charges have to be balanced)
- Physical properties:
    - high melting points (strong ionic bonds, lots of energy needed)
    - soluble in water
    - conduct electricity in solution or when molten (ions can move)
- Examples: NaCl, $MgCl_2$

**Ionic bond: Electrostatic attraction between oppositely charged ions**

$$Na^+ \ Cl^- \ Na^+ \ Cl^- \ Na^+ \ Cl^-$$
$$Cl^- \ Na^+ \ Cl^- \ Na^+ \ Cl^- \ Na^+$$
$$Na^+ \ Cl^- \ Na^+ \ Cl^- \ Na^+ \ Cl^-$$
$$Cl^- \ Na^+ \ Cl^- \ Na^+ \ Cl^- \ Na^+$$

**Covalent compounds - Molecules: Non-metals**
- Collection of atoms
- 'Dot-and Cross' diagram: overlapping circles for bonds
- Different shapes
- Formula tells which atoms are directly connected to each other
- Physical properties:
    - low melting point (weak intermolecular forces, less energy needed)
    - not soluble in water
    - not conducting electricity
- Examples: $CH_4$, $H_2O$

**Covalent bond:** **Strong electrostatic attraction between two nuclei (+) and the shared pair of electrons (-)** -> *sharing a pair of electrons*

Dative covalent bond: **both electrons** of the covalent bond come from **one atom** (arrow instead of dash) e.g. $NH_4^+$

# Shapes of Molecules I

Theory (five points)

Shapes of molecules:

One central atom with 2 partners

One central atom with 3 partners

One central atom with 4 partners

One central atom with 3 partners & 1 lone pair of electrons

## Shapes of molecules

**Electron-Pair Repulsion Theory:**
- Negative charges of electron pairs in covalent bonds and in lone pairs **repel**
- They try to get as far apart as possible
- Lone pairs of electrons on the central atom repel more (closer to atom) => smaller bond angle
- **Shape depends on number of electron pairs** (bonds, lone pairs)
- A double bond counts as a single bond (one electron pair)

**One central atom with 2 partners (electron pairs):**

$O = C = O$

180°

=> **linear, 180°**, $CO_2$, $BeCl_2$

**One central atom with 3 partners:**

F
F
B
120°
F

=> **trigonal planar, 120°**, $BF_3$

**One central atom with 4 partners:**

109.5°
H
C
H
H
H

H
N$^+$
H
H
H

=> **tetrahedral, 109.5°**, $CH_4$, $NH_4^+$
-> draw straight-line-bonds next to each other

**One central atom with 3 partners & 1 lone pair of electrons:**

N
H
H
H
107°

=> **trigonal pyramidal, 107°**, $NH_3$, $SO_3^{2-}$

# Shapes of Molecules II

One central atom with 2 partners & 2 lone pairs of electrons

One central atom with 5 partners

One central atom with 6 partners

How to get other examples

How to calculate number of lone electrons

Tip

**One central atom with 2 partners & 2 lone pairs of electrons:**

$$104.5°$$

=> bent/non-linear, 104.5°, $H_2O$

**One central atom with 5 partners:**

=> trigonal bipyramidal, 120° & 90°, $PCl_5$

**One central atom with 6 partners:**

=> octahedral, 90°, $SF_6$

To get other examples: use a different element from the same group as the central atom and keep same partners, e.g. $PH_3$ for $NH_3$

Number of lone electrons = number of outer electrons – number of bonds

--> use the expression 'electron pairs' (bonds, lone pairs) instead of 'partners' in exam (treat double bonds like single bonds)

# Electronegativity
# &
# Ionisation Energy

Definition of electronegativity

Properties of electronegativity (four points)

Definition of $1^{st}$ ionisation energy

Reactivity (two points)

Reaction equations of $1^{st}$ and $2^{nd}$ ionisation energies

Difference between $2^{nd}$ and $1^{st}$ ionisation energies (three points)

Big jump

Drops in $1^{st}$ ionisation energies with reasons

Trends across period (three points)

Trends down group (four points)

## Electronegativity

**Definition: Ability of an atom to attract electrons in a covalent bond**

- Fluorine most electronegative element
- Elements closer to F: more electronegative
- Large differences in electronegativity result in ionic compounds
- Small differences result in covalent compounds

## Ionisation Energy

**Definition of 1st Ionisation Energy:** Energy required to remove one electron from **one mole** of **gaseous** atoms [kJ/mol]

**Reactivity**
- decreases down Halogen group (want to gain one electron)
- increases down Alkali group (want to lose one electron)

**1st Ionisation energy:**      $O_{(g)} \rightarrow O^+_{(g)} + e^-$

**2nd Ionisation energy:**      $O^+_{(g)} \rightarrow O^{2+}_{(g)} + e^-$

**2nd Ionisation energy larger than 1st Ionisation energy**
- increasingly positive ion
- less repulsion amongst remaining electrons
- smaller ions

**Big jump** when new shell is broken into => closer to the nucleus

**Drop in 1st ionisation energy between Groups 2 (Be) and 3 (B)**
-> start of p-subshell, which is further away from nucleus
-> full $2s^2$ subshell provides additional shielding
-> despite increased nuclear charge

**Drop between Groups 5 (N) and 6 (O)**
-> one orbital of the 3 p-orbitals gets filled with two electrons, which **repel** each other

## Periodic Trends of Electronegativity & Ionisation Energy

**Increases across period:**
- more protons
- same shell (smaller radius)
=> stronger nuclear attraction

**Decreases down group:**
- more shells, more distance
- more shielding
- despite more protons
=> less nuclear attraction

# Intermolecular Forces – Boiling Points

Function of intermolecular forces

Relationship between intermolecular forces and boiling points

Three types of intermolecular forces

Causes of polar bonds

Why polar bonds do not always make polar molecules

Causes and properties of temporary and induced dipoles

London forces depend on... (three points)

Three elements which form hydrogen bonds

Behaviour of the Hydrogen atom

Strength of hydrogen bond compared to other forces

How to draw hydrogen bonds

Anomalous properties of water

## Intermolecular Forces

keep molecules together
-> model to explain physical states of **molecules**: **Melting & Boiling points**

The stronger the intermolecular forces the higher the melting/boiling points
-> **more energy is required to overcome these forces of attraction**

### I) Permanent dipole-permanent dipole interactions

**Permanent dipoles** contain **polar bonds** due to different **electronegativities**
-> shift in electron density

$\delta+$  $\delta-$
H - Cl
$\delta$ means slightly (or partially)
Molecules with polar bonds can be permanent dipoles (polar molecules)

**Polar bonds do not always make polar molecules**
Symmetric arrangement where polar bonds cancel each other out results in
non polar molecule, e.g. $CO_2$

### II) Induced dipole-dipole interactions: London Forces

**Non-polar molecules** contain **non polar bonds** (equal electronegativities: $Cl_2$)

**Temporary/instantaneous dipole**
- Electron cloud moving randomly (uneven distribution)
- This temporary dipole can induce another dipole => **induced dipole**
- **Weakest intermolecular force, but found in all atoms and molecules**
- Can override Permanent dipole-permanent dipole interactions (HCl < HI)
- Can hold molecules together in a molecular lattice ($I_2$)

**Depends on:**
- **number of electrons**
- **surface area**
- **points of contact**

### III) Hydrogen Bonds

**O, F, N** (very electronegative) with an H (high charge density) bonded directly
to these atoms: -NH$_2$, -OH, HF
- Strongest inter-molecular force *(H forms weak bonds with lone pair of e⁻)*
- **Write partial charges on top and draw H-bond as dotted line between H and lone pair of electrons (bond angle 180°):**

$\delta+$  $\delta-$      $\delta+$  $\delta-$      $\delta+$  $\delta-$
H— F̈ : ······ H— F̈ : ······ H— F̈ :

**Anomalous properties of water**
-> high boiling point
-> lower density of ice because of more H-bonds than liquid water:
=> lattice structure with more space; H-bonds longer than covalent bonds

---

# Module 3 - Periodic Table and Energy (Paper 1)

## 3.1 Periodic Table

### 3.1.1 Periodicity

# Periodic Table
# &
# Periodic Trends

Arranged by...

What group and period numbers stand for

Five group names

Three blocks

Blocks are named after...

Mendeleev (two points)

Elements existing as diatomic molecules

Trend of atomic radius across period (two points)

Trends of electronegativity & ionisation energy

Melting & boiling points across period (four points)

# Periodic Table

-> arranged by proton number

**Group number**
-> number of outer electrons => determines chemical properties & reactions

**Period number**
-> number of shells

**Group Names**

| | |
|---|---|
| Gr 1 | **Alkali metals** |
| Gr 2 | **Alkaline earth metals** |
| Gr 7 | **Halogens** |
| Gr 8 | **Noble Gases** |
| Gr III – XII | **Transition metals** |

**s-block**: Group 1,2 (including H and He)
**p-block**: Group 3 – 8
**d-block**: Transition elements
-> blocks are named after the outer subshell

**Mendeleev**
- Early version of periodic table: Elements arranged by atomic mass
- Left gaps to have elements with similar chemical properties in same group

**Elements existing as diatomic molecules**
$H_2, N_2, O_2,$ **Halogens:** $F_2, Cl_2, Br_2, I_2$  *(Have No Fear Of Ice-Cold Beer)*

# Periodic Trends

**Atomic radius decreases across period**
- More protons (nuclear charge/attraction) -> electrons pulled closer
- Same shell -> no extra shielding

**Electronegativity & Ionisation energy increase across period**
-> see revision card 'Electronegativity' & Ionisation Energy'

**Melting and Boiling points across period**
- Increase for metals across period -> see revision card "Metallic Bond'
- Still increase for group 4 elements -> rev. card 'Giant Covalent Structures'
- Then increase or decrease for non-metals depending on how many atoms form simple covalent structure  (London forces) -> see revision card 'Simple Covalent Structures'
- Noble gases have lowest melting points due to existing as single atoms

# Metallic Bonding
# &
# Simple and Giant Covalent Structures

Definition of metallic bonding

Trends of melting point across period (three points)

Trends of melting point down group (one point)

Characteristics of metals

Diagram of structure


Simple covalent structures for two elements

Melting points of these elements


Definition and properties of giant covalent structures

Definition of allotropes

Three allotropes of carbon

Silica

## Metallic Bonding

**Definition: Electrostatic attraction** between metal **cations** and **delocalized electrons** from the outer shell **(sea of electrons)**
-> high melting points (large energy required to overcome strong attraction)

**Across the period higher melting points:**
- more delocalized electrons (negative charges)
- charges of cations increase: $Na^+$, $Mg^{2+}$, $Al^{3+}$
- smaller ions => **higher charge density**: ratio of charge to volume

**Down the group lower melting points:**
- more shells & greater distance

**Characteristics of metals:**
- electrical & thermal conductors (free moving electrons)
- malleable & ductile; dense, shiny & soft – only alloys are hard

Giant metallic lattice

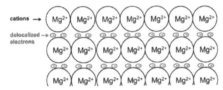

## Simple Covalent Structures (Molecules)

**Sulphur:** yellow solid, simple molecules like $S_8$ rings *or amorphous*
**Phosphorus:** white solid, simple molecules like $P_4$
-> Low melting points (less energy to overcome weak intermolecular forces)

## Giant Covalent Structures

- **Def.:** Network of covalently bonded atoms (Macromolecular Structures)
- High melting points (Large energy needed to break covalent bonds)
- C, Si => four covalent bonds (Group 4)

**Allotropes:** pure forms of the same element that differ in structure

**Allotropes of carbon:**
　　**Diamond:** 4 bonds, tetrahedral –> hard, cold, high melting point, not
　　　　conducting electricity, not soluble
　　**Graphite:** 3 bonds, trigonal planar, sheets of hexagons -> slippery, single
　　　　electrons are **delocalized** and conduct electricity, strong, lightweight
　　**Graphene:** one layer (sheet) of graphite; strong & light (composite
　　　　materials for aircrafts) -> structure and characteristics like graphite

**Silica ($SiO_2$):** tetrahedral, hard, crystals, high melting point, insoluble, not
conducting electricity => quartz, sand

# 3.1.2 Group 2

# Group 2  Alkaline Earth Metals

Reaction with water

Reaction with diluted acids

Reaction with oxygen

Oxides and Hydroxides are....

pH of hydroxide solutions

Test for sulphate

Trend down group of atomic/ionic radius

Trend down group of ionisation energy and reactivity

Trend down group of melting points

Trend down group of solubility of oxides/hydroxides

# Group 2 Alkaline Earth Metals

## Reactions of the Alkaline Earth Metals

**React with water to produce hydroxides and hydrogen gas**
$Mg_{(s)} + 2H_2O_{(l)} \rightarrow Mg(OH)_{2(aq)} + H_{2(g)}$

**React with diluted acids to produce salts and hydrogen**
$Mg + H_2SO_4 \rightarrow MgSO_4 + H_2$

**They burn in oxygen with characteristic colour**
$2Ca_{(s)} + O_{2(g)} \rightarrow 2CaO_{(s)}$ (brick red flame)
Mg -> brilliant white flame

**Group 2 oxides, hydroxides are bases (used for neutralization)**
$CaO_{(s)} + H_2O_{(l)} \rightarrow Ca(OH)_{2(aq)}$
The hydroxide ions make a solution strongly alkaline (pH 12 – 13)
-> see revision card 'Bases' and 'Acid and Bases Preparation'

**Test for sulphate (or $Ba^{2+}$ ions):** add $BaCl_2$ solution (or sulphate solution)
$Ba^{2+}_{(aq)} + SO_4^{2-}_{(aq)} \rightarrow BaSO_{4(s)}$ **white precipitate**

## Periodic Trends of Alkaline Earth Metals

**Atomic & Ionic Radius increases down** group -> more shells

**Ionisation Energy decreases down group**
**=> Reactivity increases down group**
-> see revision card 'Ionisation energy'

**Melting Points decrease down group**
-> see revision card 'Metallic bonding'

**Solubility of Group 2 oxides and hydroxides increases down group**
-> more strongly alkaline solutions

## 3.1.3 The Halogens

# Group 7  Halogens
# &
# Water Treatment

Halogens exist as...

Table with properties

Reaction with metal

Electronegativity trend down group

Reactivity trend down group

Melting points trend down group (two points)


Water treatment with chlorine

Disadvantages (two points)

Alternatives (two points)

Bleach preparation with equation and conditions

Chemical formula of bleach

## Group 7  Halogens

-> Diatomic molecules

| $F_2$ | yellow gas | very toxic | |
|---|---|---|---|
| $Cl_2$ | green gas | toxic | bleaches litmus paper |
| $Br_2$ | red-brown liquid | toxic | |
| $I_2$ | black-purple solid | | |

**Strong oxidizing agents**
  Metal + Halogen -> Halide salts (redox)
  $2Na + Cl_2 -> 2NaCl$

**Less electronegative down group**
  -> see revision card 'Electronegativity & Ionization Enthalpy'

**Less reactive down group**
  -> see revision card 'Electronegativity & Ionization Enthalpy'

**Melting/boiling point increase down group**
  • larger molecules
  • more electrons
  -> stronger London forces

## Water treatment

**Water treatment with chlorine (drinking water/swimming pool)**
$Cl_2 + H_2O \rightleftarrows HClO + HCl$ -> Disproportionation -> see revision card
  $\quad 0 \qquad\qquad\quad +1 \qquad -1$

HClO chloric(I) acid *(hypochlorous acid)* -> dissociates into $H^+$ and $ClO^-$ ions
$ClO^-$ chlorate(I) ion is strong oxidising agent which kills bacteria and algae

**Disadvantages**
  • $Cl_2$ harmful and toxic -> irritates respiratory system; liquid chlorine burns skin/eyes
  • $Cl_2$ reacts with organic compounds to form chlorinated hydrocarbons -> carcinogenic

**Alternatives**
  • **Ozone ($O_3$):** strong oxidising agent, expensive, instable
  • **UV-light:** damaging bacterial DNA, less effective in cloudy water

**Bleach Preparation**
$Cl_2 + 2NaOH -> NaClO + NaCl + H_2O$ -> Disproportionation
Condition: cold, dilute sodiumhydroxide

**Bleach: NaClO Sodium chlorate(I)** - strong oxidising agent (disinfectant)

# Halides
# &
# Displacement Reaction

Tests for halide ions with reaction equation and table

Reducing agent trend down group

Properties of hydrogen halides (two points)

Tests for hydrogen halides

Displacement reaction with equation and table (four points)

## Halides (Practical)

**Test for Halide Ions**

-> with acidified $AgNO_3$ solution

Acid $HNO_3$ removes carbonates & sulphates preventing false positives

$$Ag^+_{(aq)} + X^-_{(aq)} \rightarrow AgX_{(s)}$$

| Halide ($X^-$) | Precipitate | Dissolves in | |
|---|---|---|---|
| $F^-$ | - | | |
| $Cl^-$ | white | diluted $NH_3$ | *(complex)* |
| $Br^-$ | cream | conc $NH_3$ | *(complex)* |
| $I^-$ | yellow | insoluble | |

**Reducing agent**
-> power increases down group (more shells, more shielding)

**Hydrogen Halides**
- Colourless acidic gases
- Turn blue litmus paper red
- **Test for HCl or any other hydrogen halide (HX):**
  $$NH_{3(g)} + HCl_{(g)} \rightarrow NH_4Cl_{(s)} \rightarrow \textbf{white fumes}$$

## Displacement Reaction

- to identify halide ions
- more reactive halogen displaces (oxidises) the ion of the less reactive
  -> higher up in group => higher oxidizing strength
- special type of redox reaction
- after the reaction, shake solution with hexane or cyclohexane to get stronger colour (non-polar solvent; better for dissolving halogen)

$$\underset{0}{Cl_2} + 2\underset{-1}{Br^-} \rightarrow \underset{0}{Br_2} + 2\underset{-1}{Cl^-}$$

| | Water | Hexane |
|---|---|---|
| $F_2$ yellow gas | - | - |
| $Cl_2$ green gas | colourless | pale green |
| $Br_2$ red-brown liquid | yellow/orange | orange/red |
| $I_2$ black-purple solid | brown | pink/purple |

# 3.1.4 Qualitative Analysis

# Tests for Ions
# &
# Solubility

Tests for carbonates, $CO_2$, sulphates, ammonium & halides

Definition and characteristics of qualitative tests
Definition and characteristic of quantitative tests

How soluble a salt is depends on…
Common insoluble salts (four points)
Common soluble salts (two points)
Solvents (two points)

## Test for Ions (Qualitative Analysis) (Practical)

**Carbonates:** $CO_3^{2-} + 2H^+ \rightarrow H_2O + CO_2$    fizzing, **carbonate disappears**

**Test for $CO_2$ (limewater test):**
$Ca(OH)_{2(aq)} + CO_{2(g)} \rightarrow CaCO_{3(s)} + H_2O_{(l)}$
limewater turns **cloudy (precipitation)** in presence of $CO_2$

**Sulphate:**    $Ba^{2+}_{(aq)} + SO_4^{2-}_{(aq)} \rightarrow BaSO_{4(s)}$    **white precipitate**

**Ammonium:** $NH_4^+ + OH^- \rightarrow H_2O + NH_3$    **litmus:** red -> blue

**Halides:**    $Ag^+_{(aq)} + X^-_{(aq)} \rightarrow AgX_{(s)}$    **precipitate**

$X^-$: halide ion ($Cl^-$, $Br^-$, $I^-$)

-> see revision card 'Halides'

**Qualitative Tests:** measure physical qualities, e.g. colours, fizzing, precipitates
-> just give yes/no answers
-> subjective, therefore harder to reproduce

**Quantitative Tests:** measure numerical data, e.g. mass, volume, time etc.
-> give exact numbers

## Solubility

How soluble a salt is depends on its characteristics *($K_{sp}$ - solubility product constant)* and cannot usually be predicted from its chemical formula, but can be experimentally determined.

**Common insoluble salts:**
- silver halides
- barium sulfate
- most carbonates - except sodium, potassium, ammonium carbonates
- metal oxides

**Common soluble salts:**
- most **hydrogen carbonates** like **$NaHCO_3$** (baking soda)
- most sodium salts

**Solvents:**
- salts and polar molecules are soluble in polar solvents like water
- non polar molecules like halogens or hydrocarbons are soluble in non-polar solvents like cyclohexane

# 3.2 Physical Chemistry

## 3.2.1 Enthalpy Changes

# Enthalpy Changes – Definitions
# &
# Bond Enthalpies

Definitions of exothermic/endothermic

Definition of enthalpy change

Definitions of standard enthalpy change of:

Reaction

Formation

Combustion

Neutralisation

Two equations to calculate $\Delta H_r$ from bond enthalpies

Definition of bond dissociation enthalpy

Definition of average bond enthalpy

Two rules about bond forming and breaking

Exothermic/endothermic in relation to bond enthalpies

# Enthalpy Changes - Definitions

**Exothermic**  $-\Delta H_r$ negative: energy released into surroundings
-> heat up

**Endothermic**  $+\Delta H_r$ positive: energy taken from surroundings
-> cool down

**Enthalpy change:** Heat change in a reaction at constant pressure [**KJ mol$^{-1}$**]

**Standard enthalpy change** $^{\Theta}$: under standard conditions: **100 kPa, 298 K**

~ **of reaction $\Delta H_r^{\Theta}$**: the enthalpy change when the reaction occurs in the **molar quantities** shown in the **chemical equation**, under **standard conditions** in their **standard states**

~ **of formation $\Delta H_f^{\Theta}$**: the enthalpy change when **1 mole** of a **compound** is formed from its **elements** in their **standard states** under **standard conditions**
$2C_{(s)} + 3H_{2(g)} + \frac{1}{2}O_{2(g)} \rightarrow C_2H_5OH_{(l)}$

~ **of combustion $\Delta H_c^{\Theta}$**: the enthalpy change when **1 mole** of a substance is **completely burned in oxygen** under **standard conditions,** all reactants and products being in their **standard states**

~ **of neutralisation $\Delta H_{neut}^{\Theta}$**: the enthalpy change when **1 mole of water** is formed from the neutralisation of **hydrogen ions (H$^+$)** by **hydroxide ions (OH$^-$)** under **standard conditions**
$H^+_{(aq)} + OH^-_{(aq)} \rightarrow H_2O_{(l)}$

# Bond Enthalpies

$$\Delta H_r = \Sigma H \text{ bonds broken} - \Sigma H \text{ bonds formed}$$
or
$$\Delta H_r = \Sigma H \text{ bonds (reactants)} - \Sigma H \text{ bonds (products)}$$

**Bond Dissociation Enthalpy:** Bond dissociation enthalpy per mole of gaseous compound

**Average Bond Enthalpy:** The energy needed to break **one mole** of bonds in the **gas phase**, averaged over **many different** compounds [**kJ mol$^{-1}$**]
-> **always positive** (also for bonds formed)

- Bond forming releases energy
- Bond breaking requires energy

If $\Sigma H$ bonds formed $> \Sigma H$ bonds broken $\Rightarrow$ **exothermic**

If $\Sigma H$ bonds formed $< \Sigma H$ bonds broken $\Rightarrow$ **endothermic**

-> bond enthalpies can be used to calculate enthalpy of formation (Hess cycle)

---

# Enthalpy Profile Diagrams

Definition activation energy

Enthalpy profile diagram of exothermic reaction

Enthalpy profile diagram of endothermic reaction

Tip

## Enthalpy Profile Diagrams

**Activation energy $E_a$:** minimum amount of energy needed to begin breaking reactant bonds and start a chemical reaction **(always positive)**

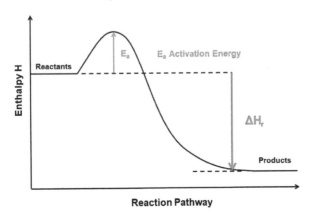

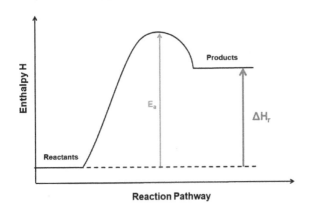

**Make sure the arrows point in the correct direction and you have labelled everything.**

# Calorimeter

Purpose

Equation for enthalpy change

Five reasons for underestimate

(Diagram of calorimeter)

Example calculation

Density of water

Three tips

## Calorimeter (-> to measure enthalpy change of a reaction) (Practical)

$$q = mc\Delta T$$

q:   enthalpy change [Joules]
m:   **mass of water [g]**
c:   specific heat capacity of water (*4.18 J g$^{-1}$ K$^{-1}$ -> data sheet*)
$\Delta T$:  temperature change [°C] **($\Delta$°C = $\Delta$°K)**

### Reasons why enthalpy change is underestimated by experiment
- Heat absorbed by container & Heat lost to surroundings
- Incomplete combustion & Evaporation of volatile fuel
- Non-standard conditions

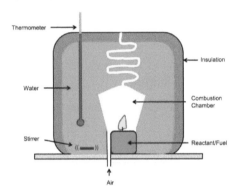

### Example Calculation - Neutralisation
30 cm$^3$ of 0.80 mol dm$^{-3}$ HCl were neutralised with 20 cm$^3$ of 1.2 mol dm$^{-3}$ NaOH. The temperature of the solutions increased from 20 °C to 26 °C. What is the standard enthalpy change of neutralization for this reaction?

$$HCl + NaOH \rightarrow NaCl + H_2O$$

Total volume of solution:    20 cm$^3$ + 30 cm$^3$ = 50 cm$^3$
**Density of water:**           **1 g cm$^{-3}$**          **density $\rho$ = m/V**
Mass of water:           50 cm$^3$ x 1 g cm$^{-3}$ = 50 g

$$q = mc\Delta T$$
$$q = 50 \text{ g} \times 4.18 \text{ J g}^{-1} \text{ K}^{-1} \times 6 \text{ K} = 1254 \text{ J}$$

Moles water formed:  n = 0.03 dm$^3$ x 0.8 mol dm$^{-3}$ = 0.024 moles

Standard enthalpy change of neutralization:
**-> divide by the number of moles reacted**

$$H_{neut}^{\ominus} = q / n = 1254 \text{ J} / 0.024 \text{ moles} = -52 \text{ kJ mol}^{-1}$$

**If temperature has increased -> exothermic reaction**
**=> put negative sign in front**

**If temperature has decreased -> endothermic reaction**
**=> put positive sign in front**

# Hess's Law

Definition

Purpose

Equation

Two rules

Three rules for triangles

Example Calculation

## Hess's law

**The total enthalpy change for a reaction is independent of the route taken** *(as long as the initial and final conditions are the same).*

-> To calculate enthalpy changes for unknown reactions from known reactions (e.g. reaction enthalpies from formation enthalpies)

$$\Delta H_{r,c} = \Sigma \Delta H_f \text{ (products)} - \Sigma \Delta H_f \text{ (reactants)}$$

$\Delta H_{r,c}$ : Enthalpy change of reaction or combustion [kJ mol$^{-1}$]
$\Delta H_f$ : Enthalpy change of formation [kJ mol$^{-1}$]
$\Delta H_r^{\ominus}$: Standard enthalpy change of reaction

- **Elements like $O_2$ have no formation enthalpy (zero)**
- **multiply formation enthalpies with mole numbers from reaction**

**Triangles/arrows,**
Add enthalpies ($\Delta H_2$, $\Delta H_3$) while going to the same products (endpoint) of the unknown enthalpy $\Delta H_1$ by using the alternative route:
**going along arrow -> positive sign for enthalpy**
**going against arrow ->** negative **sign for enthalpy**

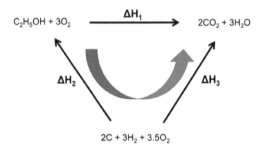

$$\Delta H_1 = -\Delta H_2 + \Delta H_3$$

**Example Calculation for standard enthalpy change of combustion for ethanol:**

$\Delta H_f^{\ominus} (CO_2) =$      -394 kJ mol$^{-1}$
$\Delta H_f^{\ominus} (H_2O) =$      -286 kJ mol$^{-1}$
$\Delta H_f^{\ominus} (C_2H_5OH) =$      -277 kJ mol$^{-1}$
$\Delta H_f^{\ominus} (O_2) =$      0 kJ mol$^{-1}$

$\Delta H_{r,c}^{\ominus}$    $= \Sigma \Delta H_f \text{ (products)}$    $-$    $\Sigma \Delta H_f \text{ (reactants)}$

$\Delta H_c^{\ominus}$    $= [(2 \text{x} -394) + (3 \text{x} -286)]$    $-$    $[-277]$      | kJ mol$^{-1}$

       $= \mathbf{-1369}$ kJ mol$^{-1}$

# Rates of Reactions

Rates depend on... (five points)

Definition & equation

Graph shows....

Four measurement methods

Collision theory (four points)

Maxwell-Boltzmann Distribution for temperature increase

Maxwell-Boltzmann Distribution with and without catalyst

Tip

Restriction of Maxwell-Boltzmann distribution

Properties of distribution curves for different concentrations

## Rates of Reactions (Practical)

**Rates (speed) depend on**
- temperature
- surface area (size of particles)
- catalyst
- concentrations of reactants (or solvent)
- pressure for gases

**Rate of reaction:** change of concentration (product or reactant) over time

$$r = \frac{\Delta c}{\Delta t}$$

**Graph:** shows increase/decrease over time

**Measurement**
- Precipitation (measure time until marker disappears)
- Change in mass when gas given off (balance)
- Volume of gas given off (syringe)
- Titration (put samples on ice to stop reaction)

**Collision Theory**
- Higher temperature -> faster => more successful collisions: $E_{kin} > E_a$.
- Higher concentration -> successful collisions more likely.
- Larger surface area -> particles can access more area.
- Catalyst -> see revision card 'Catalyst'.

**Maxwell-Bolzmann Distribution (of kinetic energy of all gas particles)**

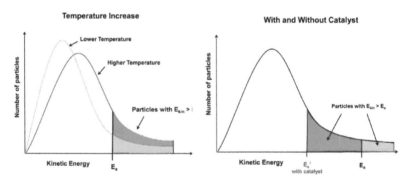

- Graphs should not touch y-axis
- Maxwell Boltzmann distribution applies to gases only
- Distribution curves for different concentrations have the same shape:
  Curve for higher concentration above the lower one => more molecules
  exceeding activation energy

# Calculate Rates of Reactions

From data table

From concentration time graphs (three points)

Graph of initial rates method

## Calculate Rates of Reactions (Practical)

### 1) From data table calculate rate:

$$r = \frac{\Delta c}{\Delta t}$$

**r:** rate of reaction $[\text{mol dm}^{-3} \text{ s}^{-1}]$
**$\Delta c$:** difference of concentrations $[\text{mol dm}^{-3}]$
**$\Delta t$:** difference in time $[\text{s}]$

### 2) From Concentration time graph:

- **Use the** slope equation $(m=\Delta y/\Delta x)$ **to calculate the gradient of a linear graph**
- **For a curved graph calculate the gradient of a tangent**
- **Initial rate method:** draw tangent through concentration at 0 s

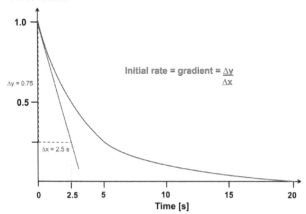

**Initial rates method for reactant A**

-> can also choose another time point t and draw tangent through it

---

# Catalyst

Definition

Homogeneous and heterogeneous catalysts with examples

Effect of catalyst on equilibrium

Catalysts save...

(Catalyst poison)

Four steps of catalyst mechanism with diagram

Enthalpy profile diagram with and without catalyst

## Catalyst

**Def.**: Increases rate of reaction by **lowering activation energy** (more successful collisions) and providing an **alternative reaction pathway**. Catalysts are **not used up** during the reactions **(unchanged).**

- **homogenous catalyst** => same physical state as the reactants; forms intermediates, e.g. enzymes/substrate (aq/aq) or Cl & Ozone (g/g)
- **heterogeneous catalyst** => different physical states
  catalytic converter Pt/Rh (s/g) in car burns hydrocarbons and:
  $2CO + 2NO \rightarrow 2CO_2 + N_2$        **CO & NO are toxic**
  other examples for heterogeneous catalyst: Ni, Fe, $V_2O_5$
- **does not change chemical equilibrium**
- catalysts save energy and costs by lowering reaction temperature/pressure and increasing reaction speed
- *Catalyst poison: binds stronger to catalyst than reactant -> blocking surface*
- **Mechanism for solid catalyst:** $H_2 + Cl_2 \rightarrow 2HCl$
  - **adsorption** (not absorption) of reactants ($H_2$, $Cl_2$) at catalyst surface
  - this **weakens bonds** in reactants (lowers activation energy)
  - **new bonds** of products (H-Cl) are formed
  - **desorption** of products (HCl) after reaction.

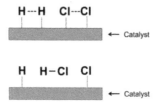

## Enthalpy profile diagram of exothermic reaction with and without catalyst

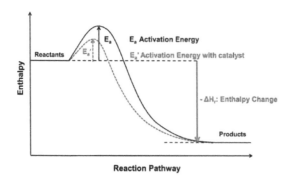

# 3.2.3 Chemical Equilibrium

# Equilibrium and Reversible Reactions

Definition of reversible reaction

Definition of dynamic equilibrium (three points)

Application

Le Chetallier

Haber process with change of conditions

Effect of catalyst on chemical equilibrium

Equilibrium law for a general reaction equation

Equilibrium constant (six points):

The larger $K_c$ ...

Equilibrium constant depends on...

When temperature is increased...

For exothermic reactions...

Units of $K_c$

How does change of concentrations affect $K_c$?

# Equilibrium and Reversible Reactions (Practical)

**Reversible reaction:** products convert back to reactants (reaction goes both ways) -> incomplete reaction => draw double arrow: ⇄

**Dynamic equilibrium (steady state)**
**-> rates of the forward and reverse reactions are equal**
- both reactions still going on; balance => low percentage of product
- **concentrations** of reactants and products remain **constant**
- only in **closed system**

-> important for yield in chemical industry

**Le Chetallier: When the conditions of a system at equilibrium change, the position of the equilibrium shifts in the direction that opposes the change**

**Ammonia manufacture (Haber-process):** iron catalyst *(200 atm, 450 °C)*

$$N_{2(g)} + 3H_{2(g)} \rightleftharpoons 2NH_{3(g)} \qquad \Delta H = -93 \ kJ/mol \ (exothermic)$$

\+ pressure      -> shifts to the side with less moles gas (here to the right)
\+ heat         -> shifts in the direction of endothermic process (here to left)
\+ concentration reactants    -> shifts to right
\- concentration products     -> shifts to right

**=> Catalyst does not change equilibrium but increases rate of both reactions (equilibrium is reached faster)**

**Equilibrium Equation**

$$aA + bB \rightleftharpoons cC + dD$$

**Equilibrium law**

$$K_c = \frac{[C]^c \, [D]^d}{[A]^a [B]^b}$$

[ ]: concentration

**$K_c$: equilibrium constant**
- the larger $K_c$ the more yield ($K_c > 1$ more products, $K_c < 1$ more reactants)
- **$K_c$ only temperature dependent**
- when temperature is increased then $K_c$ increases for endothermic reactions and decreases for exothermic reactions
- for exothermic reactions: compromise between rate and yield needed
- **need to calculate units of $K_c$** by cancelling out units of concentration
- if concentration of [C] or [D] is increased *(numerator)*, concentration of [A] and [B] must also increase *(denominator)* to keep $K_c$ constant (equilibrium moves to the left) => $K_c$ stays constant

---

# Module 4 - Core Organic Chemistry (Paper 2)

## 4.1 Basic Concepts and Hydrocarbons

## 4.1.1 Basic Concepts of Organic Chemistry

# Naming Rules for Organic Compounds
# &
# Types of Organic Formulae

Seven naming rules

Tip

Example

Types of formulae for 2-methylpentan-1-ol:

Molecular

General

Structural

Displayed

Skeletal

## Naming Rules (Nomenclature IUPAC)

- Longest chain –> forms the middle or beginning of the name (pentan-2-ol)
- Choose longest chain with most side-chains
- **Numbering carbons**: lowest number for functional groups/side chains
- Side-chains (alkyl groups): Methyl, Ethyl, Propyl, Butyl,…
  –> put at beginning of name with carbon number and dash in front (**3-ethyl-2,4-dimethyl**pentane)
- Alphabetical order for alkyl side chains (disregard di, tri, …)
  (3-ethyl-2,4-dimethylpentane)
- Multiple side-chains/functional groups: di, tri, tetra, …(2, 3, 4,…)
- Main functional group –> ending of name  (pentan-2-ol)

**Never put an alkyl side-chain (branched chain) on first or last carbon of a structural formula (creates not an isomer, just makes the chain longer)**

**Example:**

3-ethyl-2,4-dimethylpentan-2-ol

## Types of Organic Formulae

2-methylpentan-1-ol:

**Molecular formula:** $C_6H_{14}O$               (do not write $C_6H_{13}OH$)

**General formula** for all alcohols: $C_nH_{2n+1}OH$

**Structural formula:** $CH_3CH_2CH_2CH(CH_3)CH_2OH$

**Displayed formula**/structural formula (all bonds must be drawn incl. O-H):

**Skeletal formula:**

# Functional Groups

Definition of functional group

Alkene

Haloalkane

Alcohol

Aldehyde with tip

Ketone

Carboxylic acid

Ester

(Ether)

Amine

(Amide)

(Nitro)

## Functional groups

**Definition:** Group of atoms in a molecule which is responsible for the reaction

R (residue): alkyl-group $C_nH_{2n+1}$: -$CH_3$ (methyl), -$C_2H_5$ (ethyl), -$C_3H_7$ (propyl),...

Alkene                     $R-CH=CH-R$

Haloalkane                 R-X

Alcohol                    R-OH

Aldehyde

$$R-C\overset{\displaystyle O}{\underset{H}{\big\|}}$$

**Structural formula for aldehyde: RCHO**          **Do not write: RCOH**

Ketone

$$R^1-C\overset{\displaystyle O}{\underset{R^2}{\big\|}}$$

Carboxylic Acid

$$R-C\overset{\displaystyle O}{\underset{OH}{\big\|}}$$

Ester

$$R^1-C\overset{\displaystyle O}{\underset{O-R^2}{\big\|}}$$

*Ether*                    $R^1\text{-}O\text{-}R^2$

Amine                      $R-NH_2$

*Amide / Peptide (Year 2)*

$$R^1-C\overset{\displaystyle O}{\underset{NH-R^2}{\big\|}}$$

*Nitro*                    $R\text{-}NO_2$

# Three Main Types of Organic Reactions
# &
# Mechanisms


Three main types of organic reactions with examples
(Two inorganic reaction types)

Three main reaction mechanisms with word explanations
Definition and examples (two points) of electrophiles
Definition, characteristic and examples of nucleophiles


Definition of hydrolysis
Definition of condensation

## Three Main Types of Organic Reactions

**Substitution**          (e.g. haloalkane with $OH^-$)

**Elimination**          (e.g. dehydration of alcohol)

**Addition**          (e.g. HX on double bond of alkenes)

(Oxidation/Reduction -> inorganic)
(acid base reaction / salt formation -> inorganic)

## Three Main Organic Reaction Mechanisms

**electrophilic**     (likes electrons/negative charges)

**nucleophilic**     (likes positive charges)

**radical**     (unpaired electron, very aggressive)

## Electrophiles & Nucleophiles

**Electrophiles**
-> **electron pair acceptors**
- Cations: $H^+$, $CH_3CO^+$, $CH_3^+$, $X^+$
- or induced dipole molecules like halogens $X_2$ ($Br_2$)

**Nucleophiles**
-> **electron pair donors**
-> **possess at least one lone pair of electrons (ideally anions)**
- $OH^-$, $H_2O$, $CN^-$, $X^-$, $H^-$, $NH_3$, $R\text{-}OH$

## Hydrolysis & Condensation

**Hydrolysis:**
breaking of covalent bonds by reaction with water (or adding $H^+/OH^-$)

**Condensation:**
reaction in which two molecules combine to form a larger one and in which
water or another small molecule (HCl, methanol) is formed (lost)

# Alkanes
# &
# Terms

Definition of alkanes

Homologues series with general formula and physical states

Reactions of alkanes (two points)

Difference in boiling points between branched/unbranched

Application

Incomplete Combustion

Preparation

Terms:

Homologues series

Aliphatic

Alicyclic

Aromatic

Cycloalkanes

## Alkanes

Saturated hydrocarbons (only single C-C bonds, only hydrogen and carbon)

**Homologues series of alkanes: $C_n H_{2n+2}$**

| | |
|---|---|
| Methane, Ethane, Propane, Butane | -> gases |
| Pentane, Hexane, Heptane, Octane, Nonane, Decane | -> liquids |
| from $C_{18}$ | -> solid |

- unreactive (non-polar bonds)
- only other organic reactions: **radical substitution**/*elimination*
- branched isomers have lower boiling point than unbranched:
  - less surface area of contact
  - weaker London forces
  - less energy required to overcome London forces

### Application

Fuel –> Burning/combustion with $O_2$: $CO_2 + H_2O$
Limited supply of $O_2$ leads to incomplete combustion:
=> unburned hydrocarbons & CO (toxic; blocks haemoglobin)

### Preparation

From crude oil

## Terms

**Homologues series:** a group of compounds with the same general formula and the same functional group. They differ by a 'CH$_2$' group.

**Aliphatic:** a hydrocarbon joined together in straight chains, branched chains or non-aromatic rings.

**Alicyclic:** an aliphatic compound arranged in non-aromatic rings with or without side chains.

**Aromatic:** an organic compound containing a benzene ring, e.g. benzene and its derivatives.

**Cycloalkane:** a cyclic alkane, e.g. cyclohexane $C_6H_{12}$

# Radical Substitution in Alkanes

Definition of radical

Two types of fission

Curly arrows (two points)

Tip

Three steps of radical substitution with equations

Overall reaction (methane + chlorine)

## Radical Substitution in Alkanes

**Radical:** species with unpaired electron

**Homolytic fission:** each atom receives one bond electron, radicals are formed

$$Cl \overset{\frown\frown}{-} Cl \quad \xrightarrow{UV} \quad Cl\cdot \;+\; Cl\cdot$$

**Heterolytic fission:** one atom receives both bond electrons, ions are formed

$$Cl-Cl \quad \overset{\frown}{\rightarrow} \quad Cl^- \;+\; Cl^+$$

**Curly arrows**
- **full headed - movement of a pair of electrons**
- **half headed - movement of a single electron**

**Arrow has to start from a bond or a lone pair of electrons (single electron).**

**I) Initiation**

$$Cl - Cl \quad \xrightarrow{UV} \quad Cl\cdot \;+\; Cl\cdot$$

A few radicals are formed by **photodissociation** (most of $Cl_2$ still intact)

**II) Propagation (chain reaction)**

$$H-\underset{H}{\overset{H}{C}}-H \;+\; Cl\cdot \quad \longrightarrow \quad CH_3\cdot \;+\; HCl$$

$$CH_3\cdot \;+\; Cl-Cl \quad \longrightarrow \quad H_3C-Cl \;+\; Cl\cdot$$

- Cl-radical acts as a **catalyst**
- Radical substitution of H atoms with halogen atoms => haloalkanes
- Chain reaction continues until all H are substituted
  => **mixture of products**: monochloro-, dichloro-, trichloromethane and tetrachloromethane (can be separated by distillation)

**III) Termination**

$$Cl\cdot \;+\; Cl\cdot \quad \longrightarrow \quad Cl-Cl$$

$$CH_3\cdot \;+\; CH_3\cdot \quad \longrightarrow \quad H_3C-CH_3$$

$$CH_3\cdot \;+\; Cl\cdot \quad \longrightarrow \quad H_3C-Cl$$

**Overall reaction**

$$CH_4 \;+\; Cl_2 \;\rightarrow\; CH_3Cl \;+\; HCl$$

# 4.1.3 Alkenes

# Alkenes – Reaction with Halogens

Definition

General formula with tip

Preparation

Naming

Characteristics of double bond

Reactions of alkenes

Mechanism of halogenation reaction

Tip

Test for alkenes

## Alkenes – Reaction with Halogens

**Definitions:** Unsaturated hydrocarbons (C=C double bonds) -> reactive

**General Formula:** $C_nH_{2n}$ -> **same as cyclic Alkanes**

**Preparation:** from alcohols by elimination reaction *or from crude oil*

**Naming:**

$$H_3\underset{1}{C}—\underset{2}{CH}=\underset{3}{CH}—\underset{4}{CH_3}$$

but-2-ene

**Double bond: high electron density** => good target for **electrophilic Addition**

**Reactions:**

**Halogenation – electrophilic Addition**

**Addition of Halogens ($X_2$: $F_2$, $Cl_2$, $Br_2$, $I_2$)**

Alkene + $X_2$ -> Dihaloalkane

-> bromine (brown-red) gets decolourised

**Conditions:** spontaneous at RT (room temperature)

**Mechanism:**

| Induced dipole | Carbocation | 1,2 dibromoethane |
| --- | --- | --- |
| -> heterolytic fission | | |

**Halogen atoms bind only to the carbons from the double bond**

**Test for alkenes: (Practical)**

Shake with bromine water at room temperature (RT): orange -> colourless

# Alkenes - Addition of Hydrogen Halides
# &
# Hydration and Hydrogenation

Overall reaction equation for addition of hydrogen halides

Mechanism of hydrogen halide addition

Markovnikov's rule with reason


Hydration reaction

Conditions for steam hydration

Method for increasing yield of this reaction


Equation for hydrogenation reaction

Conditions

Application

## Alkenes - Addition of Hydrogen Halides

Alkene + HX -> Halogenoalkane (monosubstituted)

**Mechanism:**

permanent dipole          secondary carbocation          2-bromopropane
                                                         **(major)**

1-bromopropane
**(minor product)**

**Markovnikov's rule for electrophilic Addition on unsymmetrical alkene with H-X:**
Halide $(X^-)$ will go to carbon with more alkyl groups and $H^+$ will go to carbon with less alkyl groups
-> also applies to addition of water: OH goes to carbon with more alkyl groups

**Reason:** Alkyl groups stabilize carbocation by pushing electrons down *(Inductive effect):* primary < secondary < tertiary

## Hydration (electrophilic addition, hydrolysis)

Ethene + $H_2O$ ⇌ Ethanol

- **Steam Hydration to produce alcohols**
  **Conditions:** acid catalyst $H_3PO_4$ (on silica), 300 °C (exothermic), 60 atm. Equilibrium with low yield -> unreacted ethene is separated and recycled back into reactor

## Hydrogenation – Addition Reaction

Alkene + $H_2$ -> Alkane

**Conditions:** Ni catalyst, heat (150 °C)

**Application:** Manufacture of margarine from unsaturated vegetable oil

# Pi and Sigma Bonds

Bond characteristics of alkanes (three points)

Shape of Alkanes

Bond characteristics of alkenes (four points)

Shape of Alkenes

How to draw double bond (one point)

Two drawings of pi- and sigma-bonds in ethene

## Pi and Sigma bonds

### Alkanes

- all four Carbon bonds are **sigma(σ)-bonds**
- **σ-bond: the orbitals overlap in just one point (head-on) and therefore can rotate across axis**
- high bond enthalpy
- **shape:** tetrahedral

### Alkenes

- the double bond consist of **one σ-bond and one pi(π)-bond**
- **π-bond: p-orbitals of two carbons overlap in two points (sideways) so they cannot rotate (see left diagram below) => E/Z-isomerism**
  -> electron density spread out above & below nuclei
  => low bond enthalpy
- double bonds are stronger and shorter than single bonds
- they have high electron density
- **shape:** trigonal planar
- draw a line between the carbons for the σ-bond and two electron clouds above and below it to represent π-bond (see diagram below on the right)

**π- and σ-bonds in ethene**

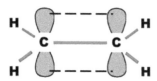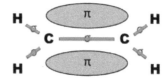

# Addition Polymers

Definition of polymers

Reaction equation forming poly(propene)

Rules for equation (three points)

Characteristics of reaction (two points)

Naming

(List of polymers with applications)

Characteristics of polymers (two points)

Disposing of polymers (three points)

Biodegradable polymers (five points)

## Addition Polymers

**Definition of polymers:** Long chain molecules of monomers *(poly – many)*

| Propene | poly(propene) |
|---------|---------------|
| Monomer | Repeating unit / Repeat unit |

**Rules**
- draw square bracket through middle of bond
- polymer chain is built only from carbons with a double bond
  -> **all other carbons form side chains**
- remember to put '**n**' on both sides of equation

**Reaction characteristics**
- **addition polymerization**
- 100 % atom economy (no waste products)

**Name from monomer**
  *Poly(ethene): cheap, strong, moulded => bags, bottles, bowls*
  *Poly(styrene): cheap, moulded, foam => outer cases, packaging*
  *PVC (polyvinyl chloride): hard, flexible => wire insulation, records*

**Characteristics**
- Not biodegradable
- Unreactive because they are saturated alkanes

**Disposing**
- Landfill
- Burning: toxic gases - HCl neutralized by bases (NaOH) in scrubbers
- Recycling: sorting -> cracking or remoulding -> organic feedstock for new plastics

**Biodegradable Polymers**
- Decompose quickly (microorganisms) -> compostable
- Made of renewable materials (starch – carbon neutral) or oil fractions
- More expensive than oil-based
- Need to be collected and separated
- Photodegradable polymers decompose when exposed to sunlight

# Types of Isomers

Two main types of isomers with definitions

Three and two subtypes respectively with examples

Conditions for E/Z isomerism

Shape of E/Z isomers

Priority rule for E/Z isomers

Tip

# Types of Isomers

## I) Structural Isomers

**Definition: same molecular formula but different structural formula**

**1) Chain-Isomers** –> chain arranged differently

$H_3C$—$CH_2$—$CH_2$—$CH_3$      $H_3C$—$\overset{\overset{\displaystyle CH_3}{|}}{C}H$—$CH_3$

      butane             2-methylpropane *(branched)*

**2) Positional Isomers** –> functional group at different positions

$H_3C$—$CH_2$—$\overset{\overset{\displaystyle OH}{|}}{C}H_2$      $H_3C$—$\overset{\overset{\displaystyle OH}{|}}{H}C$—$CH_3$

    propan-1-ol          propan-2-ol

**3) Functional Group Isomers** –> different functional groups

$H_3C$—$CH_2$—$C\overset{\displaystyle O}{\underset{\displaystyle H}{\big\lessgtr}}$      $H_3C$—$\overset{\overset{\displaystyle O}{||}}{C}$—$CH_3$

    propanal        propanone

other examples: alcohol/ether, carboxylic acid/ester

## II) Stereoisomers

**Definition: same structural formula but atoms arranged differently in space**

**1) E/Z isomerism (Cis/Trans – if just two different groups)**
  **Cond.: Double bond** (or cyclic alkane), which cannot rotate & at least
  **two different atoms/groups attached to two different carbon** atoms

  **Shape:** trigonal planar, 120°

     E *(trans)*           Z *(cis)*

  **Cahn-Ingold-Prelog:** the higher atomic number the higher priority:

       E             Z

  **For alkyl groups go further along the chain, e.g. ethyl > methyl**

**2) Optical Isomers** -> see Year 2 revision card

---

# 4.2 Alcohols, Haloalkanes and Analysis

## 4.2.1 Alcohols

# Alcohols

Three types of alcohols

Characteristics of OH-group (three points)

Dehydration reaction with conditions

Reaction with HX

Oxidising agent with colour change

Oxidising unit

Oxidation of primary, secondary and tertiary alcohols:

Equations and conditions

Combustion

## Alcohols

**Propan-1-ol**          **Propan-2-ol**          **2-Methyl-propan-2-ol**
Primary (1st degree)     Secondary (2nd)          Tertiary (3rd)
-> C with alcohol group is bonded to one, two or three other carbons

### Characteristics
- high boiling points (hydrogen bonds); *flammable*
- C-O bond **polar** (different electronegativities)
  -> **OH** good **leaving group**
  => likes to undergo **elimination & nucleophilic substitution reactions**
- acts as **nucleophile** in **esterification reactions** -> see Year 2 revision card

### Dehydration of alcohol -> Elimination reaction

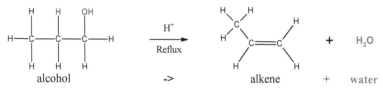

alcohol          ->          alkene     +     water

**Conditions:** heat under reflux with conc. $H_2SO_4$ or conc. $H_3PO_4$ as catalyst.
*Double bond is formed between the C with OH group and the adjacent C.*

### Nucleophilic substitution with Halide ions (NaX + $H_2SO_4$ catalyst)

**Alcohol + HX -> Haloalkane + $H_2O$**

### Oxidation of Alcohols (Practical)
- acidified ($H_2SO_4$) potassium dichromate(VI) as oxidising agent:
  orange -> green  ($K_2Cr_2O_7$ (+6) -> $Cr^{3+}$ )
- [O]: oxidising unit (gaining 2e⁻)

distillation, limited          reflux, excess

**Primary alcohol** + [O] -> **Aldehyde** + $H_2O$     + [O] -> **Carboxylic acid**

reflux, excess

**Primary alcohol + 2[O]     ->     Carboxylic acid** + $H_2O$

reflux

**Secondary alcohol + [O]     ->     Ketone** + $H_2O$

**Tertiary alcohol** -> does not get oxidised

**Burning/Combustion:**     $C_2H_5OH + 3O_2 -> 2CO_2 + 3H_2O$

# Haloalkanes

Preparation

Naming

Reactivity (three points)

Characteristics of R-X group

Mechanism with OH⁻

Three reactions with equations and conditions

## Haloalkanes (Halogenoalkanes)

Can be made by radical substitution of alkanes -> see revision card 'Radical Substitution in Alkanes'

**Naming**

2-Bromo-1-Chloropropane (alphabetically)

**Reactivity (Practical)**
- $F < Cl < Br < I$
- bigger halogen atom -> weaker C-X bond, more reactive, higher rate
- tested with hot $AgNO_3$ in ethanol -> precipitations at different rates (shorter time)

**C-X polar bond** (different electronegativities) => **X good leaving group** -> likes to undergo **nucleophilic substitution**

**Mechanism**

-> heterolytic fission of haloalkane (hydrolysis)

**Hydrolysis of Haloalkanes: nucleophilic substitution**

> $R\text{-}X + OH^- \rightarrow R\text{-}OH + X^-$        alcohol
> **Conditions:** Warm aqueous diluted sodium hydroxide solution

> $R\text{-}X + H_2O \rightarrow R\text{-}OH + HX$        alcohol
> **Conditions:** Warming

> *$R\text{-}X + 2NH_3 \rightarrow R\text{-}NH_2 + NH_4X$*        *amine (Year 2)*
> ***Conditions:*** *Heating, reflux, in ethanol*

# Ozone Layer & CFCs

Definition of radical

Function of ozone in atmosphere

Two equations for ozone formation

Equations for breakdown of ozone layer by CFCs and $NO_x$:

Initiation and Propagation reactions

Applications and properties of CFCs

Alternatives to CFCs

Bond enthalpies of different halogenes

Origins of nitrogen oxides

## Ozone Layer and CFCs

**Radical: unpaired (single) electron** (highly reactive)
=> see also revision card 'Radical Substitution on Alkanes'

**Ozone $O_3$** in upper atmosphere *(stratosphere)* protects us
-> absorbs high energy UV radiation which damages body (skin cancer)

**Ozone layer is constantly replaced:**

$$O_2 + hv\,(UV) \rightarrow O^{\cdot} + O^{\cdot}$$

$$O_2 + O^{\cdot} \leftrightarrows O_3$$

**CFCs (chlorofluorocarbons) and $NO_x$ break down ozone layer:**

**Initiation by UV radiation:**

$$CFCl_3 \rightarrow CFCl_2^{\cdot} + Cl^{\cdot} \qquad \textbf{UV (high energy in stratosphere)}$$

**Propagation:**

$$R^{\cdot} + O_3 \rightarrow RO^{\cdot} + O_2$$

$$RO^{\cdot} + O \rightarrow R^{\cdot} + O_2$$

-> Radical $R^{\cdot}$ is regenerated ($R = X^{\cdot}$ or $NO$) => catalyst

**Overall: $O_3 + O \rightarrow 2O_2$**

- CFCs were used as **coolant gas in fridges, solvents and propellants**
  They are **inert** and very stable -> live long enough to reach stratosphere, where they are photodissociated by high energy UV radiation
- **Alternatives: HCFC** (hydrochlorofluorocarbons) **& HFC & Hydrocarbons** are less stable
  -> broken down before reaching ozone layer
- bond enthalpies: C-I < C-Br < C-Cl < C-F
  => more difficult photodissociation towards C-F
- Nitrogen oxides ($NO_x$) are produced by car and aircraft engines (high temperatures)

## 4.2.3 Organic Synthesis

# Separating Funnel
# &
# Reflux Apparatus

Purpose of separating funnel

Diagram of separating funnel

Workings of separating funnel

Purpose of reflux apparatus

Diagram

Workings of reflux apparatus

## Separating funnel (Practical)

-> To separate a liquid organic phase from an aqueous phase

- During the synthesis of an organic compound, in an aqueous solution, the mixture is shaken in the separating funnel
- Pressure has to be released by opening the stopper frequently (product is volatile)
- The mixture will separate into two layers: organic phase & aqueous phase
- The organic layer is usually on top, due to its lower density
- The aqueous layer contains impurities and is drained by opening the stopper and tap
- Close the tap when the organic layer reaches it
- Transfer the organic product into a storage bottle

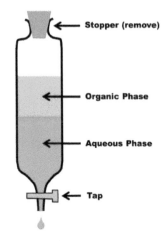

Stopper (remove)

Organic Phase

Aqueous Phase

Tap

## Reflux Apparatus (Practical)

-> To heat a reaction mixture of volatile liquids above their boiling points

- Most organic reactions need heating to boiling point.
- Volatile reactants or products would evaporate and escape as gases.
- The flask cannot be closed or it would explode.
- To prevent evaporation the gaseous compounds are condensed back into liquids, in the Liebig condenser.
- These liquids drop back into the reaction flask.
- Here they are collected (products) or continue to react (reactants).
- Anti-bumping granules smooth the boiling process by providing a surface for bubbles to form.
- Electrical heaters (heating mantel) are used to avoid naked flames which could ignite flammable organic compounds.

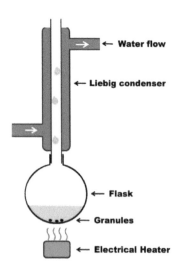

Water flow

Liebig condenser

Flask

Granules

Electrical Heater

# Distillation Apparatus
# &
# Drying with Anhydrous Salts


Purpose of Distillation Apparatus

Diagram

Description

Indication of impurities

Method to remove impurities


Purpose of drying with anhydrous salts

Description (four points)

## Distillation Apparatus (Practical)

-> To separate different fractions of a liquid mixture by boiling points

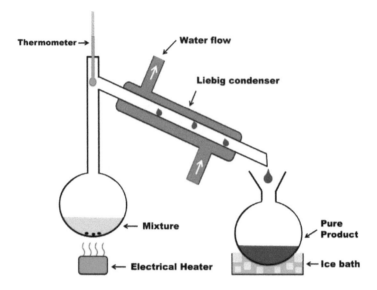

- After a reaction: mixture of products and unreacted reactants present
- The desired product is separated from the mixture by heating
- Compounds with lower boiling points evaporate first
- They condense in the Liebig-condenser and are collected
- The **cooled** collection vessel is changed when the **boiling point** of the desired product is reached (indicated by the thermometer: the temperature remains constant for a while). Cooling prevents product loss by evaporation.
- This pure product is then collected and stored
- **A boiling point higher than expected (data table) indicates impurities**
- If the product still contains impurities it can be distilled again: **Redistillation**

## Drying with Anhydrous Salts (Practical)

-> anhydrous salts are used to remove traces of water from a liquid organic product

- After separation of an organic product from the reaction mixture, with a separating funnel or distillation, it might still contain traces of water
- They are removed by adding solid anhydrous salts like $MgSO_4$ or $CaCl_2$
- The water gets incorporated into the salt as water of crystallisation
- The salt is then removed by filtration or decanting

---

# *Recrystallisation*
# &
# Synthetic Routes


*Purpose of Recrystallisation*

*Method*

*Diagram of Buchner funnel & flask*


Synthetic routes for:

Alkane, alkene, alcohol, haloalkane,

aldehyde/ketone, carboxylic acid

## Recrystallisation (Year 2) (Practical)

-> *Removes impurities from a solid compound, which is soluble at high temperatures and insoluble at low temperatures*

- *Hot solvent is added to the impure solid until it just dissolves -> saturated*
- *The solution is slowly cooled down until crystals of the product are formed*
- *The impurities remain in the solution, due to their lower concentration*
- *The pure product crystals are filtered, washed with cold solvent and dried:*
  *A Buchner funnel with filter paper and **Buchner flask** with a vacuum pump attached to the side arm are used (see diagram)*
- *The reduced pressure in the flask speeds up filtration*
- *The pure product has a higher melting point than the impure one*

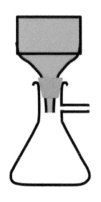

## Synthetic Routes

| Name | Group | Properties | Reactions (target for...) |
|------|-------|-----------|---------------------------|
| Alkane | C-C | unreactive non-polar | Radical Substitution, Burning |
| Alkene | C=C | high electron density | Electrophilic Addition |
| Alcohol | C-OH | polar -> good leaving group | Nucleophilic Substitution, Elimination (Dehydration) |
| Haloalkane | C-X | polar -> good leaving group | Nucleophilic Substitution |
| Aldehyde/ Ketone | C=O | polar -> bad leaving group | Oxidation of Aldehyde |
| Carboxylic acid | COOH | (proton donor) | (Acid-Base Reactions) |

-> See also Year 2 revision card 'Tips for Organic Synthesis Questions'

## 4.2.4 Analytical Techniques

# IR Spectroscopy
# &
# Greenhouse Effect

Purpose of IR spectroscopy

Workings of IR spectroscopy

Tip

Other applications (two points)

Three greenhouse gases

Workings of greenhouse gases

Mechanism of global warming (three points)

Contribution depends on (two points)

Scientific evidence for global warning (three points)

## IR Spectroscopy

-> To **identify** different types of covalent **bonds** => **functional groups**

- Absorption of IR radiation lets **bonds vibrate** (different bonds – different frequency)
- Spectrum: transmittance (%) versus wavenumber ($cm^{-1}$).
- transmittance: reverse of absorbance
- wavenumber: inverse of wavelength
- *wavenumber: the smaller the less energy*
- **State if O-H (alcohol** *3400 $cm^{-1}$* **or carboxylic acid** *2800 $cm^{-1}$*) **and C=O (carbonyl** *1700 $cm^{-1}$*) **peaks are present**
- *Data Sheet with functional groups and wavenumbers is provided in exam*

**Other applications**
- accurate **breathalyser** test for alcohol in breath of drunk drivers (evidence in law court)
  -> Ratio of OH-peak to CH-peak of Ethanol
- to monitor **air pollution** ($CO_2$, NO, $SO_2$, $CH_4$)


## Greenhouse Effect

**Greenhouse gases**
- $H_2O$, $CO_2$, $CH_4$
- absorb IR radiation -> bonds vibrate

**Mechanism**
- Earth absorbs UV/Vis light and heats up
- Heat is normally radiated back into space through IR window (IR frequencies not absorbed by atmospheric gases)
- Greenhouse gases in troposphere absorb other IR frequencies and re-emit back to earth causing global warming (rise of sea levels, climate change)

**Contribution depends on**
- How much radiation absorbed by molecules
- Concentration of gas

**Scientific evidence for global warming**
- Average temperature increased
- $CO_2$ levels increased
- Sea water more acidic ($H_2CO_3$)